THE
CLOUD
PATH

T0085846

POETRY
Where Outside the Body Is the Soul Today
Pictograph
The Nine Senses
I Go to the Ruined Place (editor, with M.L. Smoker)
Reading Novalis in Montana
Thistle
The Archival Birds

FICTION
Trees Call for What They Need
Modern Daughters and the Outlaw West

NONFICTION
Putting on the Dog
Earth Recitals
Toward the Open Field (editor)

THE
CLOUD
PATH

poems

MELISSA
KWASNY

MILKWEED EDITIONS

© 2024, Text by Melissa Kwasny
All rights reserved. Except for brief quotations in critical articles or reviews, no part of this book may be reproduced in any manner without prior written permission from the publisher: Milkweed Editions, 1011 Washington Avenue South, Suite 300, Minneapolis, Minnesota 55415. (800) 520-6455
milkweed.org

Published 2024 by Milkweed Editions
Printed in the United States of America
Cover design by Mary Austin Speaker
Cover artwork: "American Fork No. 16" by Sandra Dal Poggetto, courtesy of Echo Arts
Author photo by Bryher Herak
24 25 26 27 28   5 4 3 2 1
First Edition

Library of Congress Cataloging-in-Publication Data

Names: Kwasny, Melissa, 1954– author.
Title: The cloud path : poems / Melissa Kwasny.
Other titles: The cloud path (Compilation)
Description: First edition. | Minneapolis, Minnesota : Milkweed Editions, 2024. | Summary: "An imaginative reworking of the elegy that focuses on the difficult work of being with the dying"–- Provided by publisher.
Identifiers: LCCN 2023036703 (print) | LCCN 2023036704 (ebook) | ISBN 9781639550920 (trade paperback) | ISBN 9781639550937 (ebook)
Subjects: LCGFT: Poetry.
Classification: LCC PS3561.W447 C58 2024 (print) | LCC PS3561.W447 (ebook) | DDC 811/.54--dc23/eng/20230830
LC record available at https://lccn.loc.gov/2023036703
LC ebook record available at https://lccn.loc.gov/2023036704

Milkweed Editions is committed to ecological stewardship. We strive to align our book production practices with this principle, and to reduce the impact of our operations in the environment. We are a member of the Green Press Initiative, a nonprofit coalition of publishers, manufacturers, and authors working to protect the world's endangered forests and conserve natural resources.

for Barbara Kwasny

CONTENTS

II.

THE STONE COTTAGE

III.

THE PATH OF MELTING ICE

IV.

SLEEP PRACTICE

The most beautiful part
of your body is wherever
your mother's shadow falls.
—OCEAN VUONG

THE
CLOUD
PATH

THE CLOUD PATH

Last night, my mother's dog woke me to find her
    drenched with sweat, *passed out*,
        as we say, unreachable.

My mother, who refuses to wear her hearing aids,
    moves unhearing into her world,
        her own narrative interpretations.

Passing through:
    as needles through fine or heavy cloth
    as clouds over the mountain
    they are more transient than us
    nuages en lambeaux (torn clouds)

Six friends have died. My father has died. My grandparents,
    two cats, a beloved dog.
        Passed away, a perfect phrase,

for away is where they go. A quickness seen from the ground.
        And the *past*, which we often misuse
        or misspell.

Blue on the cloud-hem indicates pressure being released,
    a body on the down slope, misshapen.
        Relative to what stays the same so long.

Do you have moments, too, when you fear everything
        is sliding, that you are here
                on the melting ice-edge of loss,

though the pond hangs onto its ice daily,
        dry leaves skipping across the surface.
                I love that it still holds our weight.

I. GLASS VOCABULARY

the purity of paths
the simplicity of water—
                    —GENNADY AYGI

AN ASCETIC IMPULSE SURFACES, TEARS LEAVES FROM THEIR STEMS

The rains began last night, clearing the air for snow,
making the air more vulnerable and so, more accepting.
I pull the fava bean vines and lay them to mulch
in the trough, dig the purple potatoes that have scabbed.
Yesterday, I went to my old house in the mountains
to visit the wild birds, not the bush sparrows or finch
I feed here, but the delicate green flycatcher
with its white eye-ring who used to land on the banisters
like a charm. Animals have made a new trail
to the water. Allowable, no longer frightened of me.
Who are they, leaving no scat, no sign,
only a cemetery-quiet, an empty cold vault, looted
of valuables. As I have left my visionary days behind me.
Even the road I traveled is less passable.
Still an incandescent light I could not have planned for.
I used to feel omniscient as the snow.
Is there a word for layers the hay parts into when I gather
it in my arms? A word for the slump
where granite sags, in knee-buckling mud? Is there a word
for my new point of view? Surely not first-person
nor third, not domesticated or wild, something artisanal
like the potter's *clay slip*, the flautist's *embouchure*,
the painter's *palette knife,* like when I dream
my own performance but am watching it from the inside.
One of three talents you might bestow upon a child.
If god is pressure, as the occultist writes,

it's a wonder anything holds up: cloud shapes, the spindle
of branches under the weight of a ruffed grouse.
It is awful to be disappointed when one has had so much.

REREADING DION FORTUNE'S *PSYCHIC*
SELF-DEFENSE

Any act performed with intention becomes a rite,
the author claims. The trout kicks its tail, displacing sand.
One's sight must step down, through water, counting
the eccentric rungs. One must vacuum up strands of one's hair.
The teachings I was once drawn to now feel vintage,
dusty vials still on the shelves in a ghost town apothecary,
coarse remedies that might just as easily harm me.
What I know: ghosts are gray because they are merely shadows
cast from the dead. Beauty often leads to the divine.
The earth here, disturbed by miners, emits radon, some say
a cure for pain. In healing itself, can earth yield to us an influence?
The book names four conditions under which
we may meet the unseen: in places, in people, in losing one's way,
or in falling victim to illness, whether in body or mind.
I wake thinking about the corridors the ancient ones walked,
following the mammoth, the bison, then nine feet tall,
enormous herds of pronghorn whose species remains unchanged,
every square inch packed with their destinies and bones.
One settler's plow can tear up evidence of occupation
spanning thousands of years, mixing liquor bottles with spear points,
tin with obsidian, unrelinquished until worn down to a nub.
Let us at least be kind to each other. Here, at the crossroads,
which I get a glimpse of when my mother falls asleep in her chair,
arms drifting, hands circling as she mouths words I can't hear.
In *ether*, the upper region beyond the clouds.
I have gone through the fortune book and erased all the marks,
the five-pointed stars, the underlines, the marginalia

I wrote when I was young. I've thrown away the occult pamphlets
I kept for years in my car's trunk, thinking what,
that one day I would pull over and read them? The truth is
I have never had the heart for it, the danger or the risks—if one
is unprepared, under-trained, if the trick goes wrong.
And we all fall down. The dead, our true marginalia.
I was once present as I am now, walking down the same road,
past the backside of the village, the peeling houses, the ruined cars.
What was I afraid of? What defense did I need?
Just when I washed my hands of it, backed up from the ledge,
content with my small specialties—finding lost things,
remembering what someone did—the book returns, and why
wouldn't it, like stray broken threads, a spider's web I inadvertently
walk into. Nothing frightening. Nothing magical, or wrong.

SEARCHING FOR THE GLASSES YOU DROPPED
IN THE CREEK

Like reading something difficult, for instance, a novel
by Virginia Woolf, who requires we adopt her way of seeing
before proceeding with the plot, I stare so intently
into the current as it clouds and clears that when a dark shape
swerves across it I almost shout. Experiment: believe
the trout is showing me where water orbits two plates of glass,
the offering a complement to the sheer September air,
the random accident of their meeting a mirage. One night,
a little tipsy, we explored the backstreets of our small town
until we came upon the same creek, blocks from the bar.
Funny, how it had seemed the happiest thing around.
A river collects its tributaries like a heart spreads out its veins.
Ancestral path and ancestors all at once. A whole world
we can be absorbed into, like snowflakes on plowed ground.
And always, the earth will replace us. The force
of autumn is toppling the last of our hot days under the waves
or farther down, maybe into the ocean by now.
I admit, your glasses will be almost impossible to find,
like two black lines drawn on shade under the lips of stones.
They will appear, if they do appear, as something foreign,
not quite right. There is the very real possibility
that they are gone. I used to be less interested in the invisible
than in what the visible has to say. Windowpanes were useless.
Granite was fair. Still, I keep returning to the creek, as if testing
my powers: the ramparts of cottonwood, the thin tablets
of ice slipped between leaves that catch and pile at the curves.

THE WEEK OF MOVING GLASS

Did we breathe as we did it, focusing on our feet
and the ice that sometimes softened into mud?
Old, we felt the strain, our waists twisting
in odd pain in order to face each other and still walk.
So many dangers we didn't speak of,
though we each had our list, a slip, a corner hitting
a door jamb, but worse was getting lost
in the view. Sky underfoot is what it felt like,
a tilting as if I were in a plane. Clouds and blue
in a panic at being captured. If the piece
were round, it would have been more difficult.
We slid our fingertips beneath an edge, then edged
them in until we palmed it at its waist.
Like one might do for an ill person trying to stand.
I wonder how many rocks I will throw
in the river for each of my dead a year from now.
Ground glass, they say, settling in the lungs.
Glass, in its plural form: what we drink from or wear
to see. Mirror or window: what we use to see
outside the self. I am already dreaming about ways
it could cause harm: to shatter, to sliver,
to sever—a sibilance that makes me clench my teeth.
We close our eyes, try to still ourselves, balance
on our rope, extra arms poling as if they were wings.
Hoping we meet no cars, encounter no wind,
only grace in retrospect after we lower it to the floor.
Stained glass in which the color of everything
is now absorbed. Suspended: an act of death defying.

GLASS VOCABULARY

Clear footpath of the goddess, lined
with travertine, a stone the color of eggshell
boiled with onion skin, and rippled glass
that we, born in the industrial age, get to see
at last—the sky unmitigated. What does it mean
to dot your i's and cross your t's for those
too young to write *by hand*? We, in a high risk
category, fell in love on this land, cattle-
beaten juniper and the driest crumble of sage,
under a smaller sky, swirled with silver winds.
The trodden mud has hardened
after their lumbering, fractured and annealed.
The spring reaches only this far in spring.
If we never make it back to Rome—
the black-shawled women, the flower market,
the mosaics and tiles—it will be okay.
As we leap back and forth across the trickle
to avoid the gray, dead limbs, you are already
making alternate plans: what private land
to ask permission to cross, what trails within
our sphere. Village life after a lifetime of travel.
Last night, on my way to your house,
an old friend appeared at the gate, asking
silver apples of the moon, the golden apples of the sun?
Yes, Yeats, but which poem, she wanted to know.
And maybe this is all that's asked of us,
or all that we might ask—that the book opens to
the poem, that the mind finds its way, not

to a screen, but to a different kind of proficiency.
We grind blue seeds of juniper under our shoes.
Cow bones bleach in the creek, broken
and scattered. You say you like to revisit places,
to come back to them, over and over again.
Whoever you are with now, the news analyst says,
is who you will be with for the long term.
Glassed in behind the tempered, the beveled,
the opalescent or float glass, it is grief for the fragile
world that we wake to together. While a solitaire
sings at the tip of a tree, the horned lark
is invisible to me. We are older, more careful.
A day may be lost. Instead, we remember to return:
to draperies of earth that hide in their folds
the young streams, rear flank of an animal we startle.

THE SNOW GEESE PATH

We follow the loosely strung pearls of a necklace
flung against the sky   as if out of vision,

faint at first then gaining dimension, as if they were
conjured, a magic trick unraveling from the horizon,

indecipherable scripts that hold just long enough to
be form and break apart.   Terrorized by premonitions.

Our eyes are heavy from seeing. The geese lift them.
A kind of speech. We feel doomed, my brother said,

from across the country. We're trying to keep Mother
safe.   Somebody still has to go for groceries.

Last night, I dreamt the word *round*, as in a round table,
and then as noun: a round of poker or antibiotics or

drinks or song. Verb: to round a number to the highest.
One-hundred-thousand snow geese circle barren fields.

One-hundred-thousand people have now died of a virus.
We walk between two lakes, one still frozen.   One

with open water where buffleheads dive. While overhead,
snow geese float, without seeming to flap their wings,

a fly line or ellipsis extended. A distant roar that could
be their hunger or happiness.   And then it is over—

only blank sky. As if disappearance were the opposite
of infection. I mean, the blue above us seems saturated,

the bluest I have ever seen, as if sky were being cleared
of our inheritance.   A blue like in the old stories

about a people who survive: my mother long enough
to die with me beside her. My brother to gain a lucky life.

HIEROPHANT (THE ASPENS)

                                    Spring-fed spirits
of clarity. How to be clear like them, to skate among them.
In their winter lot.   How to prepare the bright leaves.

Queen-like, as in a procession.   Silent as an answer.
                        Root chorus of lower-case vowels.
A musician skims a mallet across the face of ancient gongs.

Like coming upon a room of enchantments, a row of pillars
wrapped in silver.   Or a strict number of white candles.
They allay me.

                        As if I had been taken by the hand
to a window above an alluvial plain.   Queen Anne's lace,
a carpet woven with weeds—how sorrow can overtake us.

They breathe us.   They pull our torn sleeves.
What to say to them now that my mother is failing?
Snow falling between aspen trunks seems especially quiet,

touching me like someone who favors me might.
Their catkins will soon appear overnight, sacramentalizing
the approach   where I tie my longings,

where my prayer throbs—
near the deer-borne bridge, ascending to the star schools—
my prayer to leave her here   at the edge of a grove.

THE COTTONWOOD PATH

Most metaphors are shiny, the shine a switch
from the dull side of wind-whipped leaves above us.
We sit near the creek, watching the massive trunks
sway in columns almost fluid as the grasses.
Only a matter of time, people say, before it hits us,
bad luck or disease. For now, we've entered a lull.
My mother safe in her hospital bed at home.
You here with me, though grown so thin you stumble.
Some people can feel coolness not only in touch,
but also in sound and sight. Veranda for the blackbirds,
cover for the pear-green finch, the cottonwoods
never form a forest but line up in rough silk, tertiary
home of those who live by water. Emerson spoke
of a *bird-while*, you tell me, the measure of a bird's pause,
perched just long enough to allow itself to be seen.
It was years before I could find the exact tree
where I laid the book down. Meanwhile, others had
stepped into the periphery. Once, a limb cracked
and fell into a friend's yard, so large it took her chainsaw
to remove it. Crushed under the pile of twigs
and leaves, she found the dead chicks and broken nests.
We are trying to find words for holding this kind
of disaster in mind, to sit with it, not exactly to accept it.
You shape your arms like a basket you are offering me.
And all the while, tied to snowflakes, the cotton-
wood seeds swirl, as if they were choosing where to land.

THE GLASSWING BUTTERFLY

We're not there yet, my brother says
about the dying path, day-ground crackling with stardust.

My mother's skin is nearly see-through
like the butterfly with its soldered, stained-glass wings,

fragile as a child the fairies steal, tempting her with cherries.
A thought that lets me step aside from pain.

I have always had faith in the intellectual surpremacy
of earth. Like my mother, it grows strong when he quits

beating her. This also: that often messages meant for others
come to us in our dreams, which is why

we must remember to recount them. You can ask
the tiniest birds to reveal themselves, a kinglet lost in leaves,

my mother, whom I tend to, attend, am tender to for days,
shadowing her down the hall as she grips her walker.

I slip on the blue gloves, anoint her private parts with salve,
spread honey and calendula on her bed sores,

guide her arms through her sleeves. In the face of
such intimacy, how shameless her trust in me, animal proof

that the body provides. My skin, too, grows
pocked and tattered. My heart races when I drink gin. The sky

fills suddenly with clouds. Hope for the world slipping out
of my hands, like the phone does from hers, a voice still in it.

OWL NEST

They get active in evening, my friend says,
and tuck inside if it rains. It isn't raining, but the air
is cold as emeralds. We stand in our down coats,
pointing our binoculars at the broken-off,
jagged slopes atop the giant ruin that is the tree.
"Dear Outside World," one of my students writes,
"all I can see from my window are the animals
in my backyard and the bushes that form a periphery.
I think this might be all you are for now."
An owlet risks the open and stares myopically.
Its parents enter the cloud cover above the stream.
To camouflage, to impersonate, both perpetuate
a fraud—one hides, one wears the guise of another—
the gray bark for minutes I would swear is the bird
or the bird watching us, still as wood can be.
I, too, am waiting at the threshold as my mother leaves
the earth, her presence already fading from view.
Her hands can no longer grip her spoon, her syringe.
But for whom is the world not dangerous?
My friend says he spent two hours on his stoop
in the dark, while the owls delivered countless voles
and once a snake. Three toes facing forward,
a fourth talon that can pivot back, the owlet's clutch
is already big as its head. If we can imagine
the worst beforehand, will it be easier when it comes?
My mother is feeling better. Will she live?
A fox pads into the field beyond us as if it believed
that we can't see it over the stems of last year's grass.

THE FIRST TO CHANGE

According to the Japanese poets: the scarecrow,
insect sounds, chrysanthemums, and the moon.
Here, the willow swaps its green for yellow feathers.
The emptiest, stubble fields that fill with
our large houses and roads. The so-called dead.
Or the happiest people, who have the most to lose.
The freshness of the words we use most often.
The wind today grows restless to be done with leaves.
Change sounds good when one is sick of oneself.
My mother's blood tests came back negative.
Yesterday, she thought she was going to die.
The beginning of autumn, Buson wrote. *Why is the fortune
-teller looking so surprised?* Young girls, saplings,
snap peas entangled in their vines—if to grow is to
become larger, to grow old must involve a trance,
slipping out of the body into vaster realms of memory.
If time is our own construct, why can't we build it
without beginnings or ends, with lamps, but no clocks
and no miles? My mother slips like the creek slips
through the afternoon, each day quieter, more shallow.
First to change is the moment, next the months
and years. Last, perhaps all those who fear uncertainty.

THE PORTABLE SHRINE

Gather the bones and pile them near the aspen, still in leaf.
A clavicle, a dozen fetlocks, a few big as your knee,
a thousand-pound animal reduced to what you can easily carry.
Some days there will be beer cans, underwear from a fling.
There must be forgiveness, a clearing, a space swept of debris.
Taking and giving, a crucial part of the portable shrine.
Focus. You must pause to do so, which means
you come alone, the bitter breakfast tea still on your tongue.
In your toolkit: a three-foot plume of purple fireweed
gone to smoke and seed. A book of matches, perhaps a bell.
The bell can be a cowbell, wind chimes, or the tap
of two stones, soft as the bald path you've worn between
your house and a loved one's. Add incense, candles, or ashes
from a stove. Yes, ashes, no matter whose, will build one.
Remember the old world is site-specific. Place a rock
in a shallow stream. See how many more you can balance
atop it. Hold your breath like a robin's egg, as if you
were a nest, entrusted with all things smooth, blue, and oval.
The last night you were at your mother's house, unable
to sleep, you took photos of her kitchen cabinets, her pillbox,
her matching towels, printed with flowers and leaves.
There are shrines we leave behind us, un-portable shrines.
Set a flag blowing in the wind, bow to the moon in the west,
where the herbalists rub its skin with oil of pine.
But know there are places you can approach only in the mind.

OUT OF THE WOODS

My mother is a scarecrow, a bundle
of old bones and rags, propped in a field, dreaming
on morphine. Hurrying past the carpenter
and the neighbors on their deck, head down, a prayer
flag tucked under my arm, I, too, have given up
on appearances. Amidst the record daily infections,
forcibly retired, I wear the same shabby sweater
every day, shoveling a ditch inside myself
to bury the stray hairs, which collect on the pillowcase
and clog the drains. I stand in a forest.
My brother holds the phone to my mother's ear.
I was thinking of you. What kind of thought, she says.
As if it might tell her something about her prospects.
When her voice disappears, I hear the wind.
What else have I not perceived before? Was the now-
disappeared louder, overwhelming the unperceived
or did one sound simply cancel the other out?
Unlike animals that curl, burrow deep into their pain,
heading off alone to not be bothered, very few
of us slip quietly under the veil. We say death happens
all the time, but does that mean *all the time at once*—
one way to think about our lives. Which once seemed
easy, a snowstorm watched from a warm room,
while in the woods, the trunks candle in failing light.
Redeemed by proximity to these last of religious signs,
if I believed in priests, I would confess to the pines.

BIRTH PLACE

The smell, my sister says, I can't take it. As if death
were a sin, a failure to be abstract and motherly.
Damn you, my mother shouts, who almost never swears.
Her skin aches when a feather moves across it.
My brother speaks loudly to her because she cannot hear.
I whisper less for her sake than for mine,
clasping her beautiful, poorly-mended wrist, desperate
for the few moments she still exists, the thick of it
through which I live my life. We are not born alone
but of mothers. To say we die alone is a common
view, but who knows who will meet her at the hand off?
After morphine. After the oxygen machine's heavy dirge.
Hearing is the last to go, the nurses say, after speech,
swallowing, sight. Cold we feel and our consciousness
of feeling cold. *Repressing haste, as too unholy,* we stay
up all night, locking the doors, as if protecting our grief
from the threat of those who will try to lighten it.
So many mythologies of daughters murdered or abducted,
but so few of a mother gone. The mother, perhaps,
too large for any story. Caravaggio's painting of the Virgin
splayed in exhaustion across the bed, her bodice
loosened, the mourners' heads in their hands, speaks not
of soul, but of the body. And so the painting was
condemned. We had hoped for swan wings, a serene
beating, not a gasp, the walls of the mourning room pale
as white hydrangea. Instead, there is no light here,
the music is turned off. We dress her as if she were a doll.

THE RIVER PATH

We approach the overlap of our old walk
        from the opposite direction and that makes us
mistrust the views. Is this the highest hill?
        Why can't we see the pond? The pile of bones
must be new, dragged by coyotes across the long
        fields of sage after last year's calving.
The cliffs above us we used to stand on but didn't see.
Can it really be so simple as starting elsewhere?
        Today you stop at an increase, motion
for me to go ahead, thinking to give me space to mourn
        my mother. You are smoking,
and shrinking as I leave you into a sentinel or sign
that seems too prominent, as if meaning you will be first
        to die, becoming the sudden quiet in the room.
We have convinced ourselves, Socrates said,
that we exist on the surface of earth, when we actually
        live on the bottom, amid dregs
of the densest brew, while above us, a mounting
        clarification, a light bleeding through,
soaking into us like water darkens a length of linen.
        When I think of all those who came before me,
the word generosity comes to mind. Maybe someone waited
        down by the river for my mother, too.

ELEGY

Pine-Winds, my Friends, please arrive at my gate.
That she is not here but that she was seems unbearable.
Send me a handbell for evening and one for dawn.
My wish: that we could all learn to evaporate.
Google: mother, death, angels, heaven, hell, assumption.
Her neighbors brought bouquets to her sickbed,
in which the same flowers appeared: tea roses, hibiscus,
and blue hydrangea. They brought their tiny dogs
to cheer her, lifting them to her lap. She had quit eating
a week beforehand, so fruit baskets only made her cry,
as did a child's voice, or any mention of the word *hospice*.
Did we interrupt her soul's plan? Were we obstacles
in its path, doling out drops of morphine until she slept?
My brother turning clumsy. My sister looming large.
It's okay, we kept repeating, when it was clearly not so.
If we could have sung, but our family never sang.
Once, I sent my mother lilacs, wrapped in wet newsprint,
to Florida, where it's too hot for them to grow,
though it took over a week for them to reach her. Once,
she asked me for a photo that would represent her,
but *not of her.* I took a picture of falling snow. Admittedly,
the image wasn't clear. But this is how we talked to
each other. I want to know more about dying than death,
this side of it as distinct from that of mourning.
Must it always be like hers was, a dark hallway strewn
with broken glass. Can the scene ever be swept of dread?
They say an elegy should include a catalog of flowers,
a cast of mourners, repetition of the deceased's name, anger

and accusation, though performed in a measured pace,
one that follows the progressive drama of the seasonal gods.
My mother seemed to live in a different world than ours,
her prayer jars by the dog treats, hidden in plain sight,
her journals never shared, her thoughts unwinding in spools
of words we couldn't follow. Still, we came to her
with our questions. She was the oracle of our late nights.
Perhaps my father was jealous he couldn't reach her. Perhaps
that's why he hit her, though that was never her story,
only mine. Perhaps her death was filled with light and chimes.

AFTER THE VACCINE

How should we gather, I ask you. In circles?
Outside? And what should we bring
besides the names of our dead, their photographs,
their last words, who accompanied them?
A list of postponed events? Remember, we will
all be changed. We will have to draw
each other in. There will be much to go over,
to lay out in the open. The red-shouldered hawk
that crash-landed in the sparrow bushes
and stood stunned on the walk, just long enough
for me to wheel my mother to the window.
There are other stories, aren't there, those carried
on the wind but now caught in a windbreak
of Russian olive? Stories that should fit into us
like a drawer into a chest of drawers. Or
maybe we should share what we've been given:
a bowl of apples, a pair of gray cashmere gloves
into which a seamstress slid a turquoise lining.
"Were you yourself, Phaedo, in the prison
with Socrates on the day that he drank the poison?"
the dialogue in Plato begins. Who else was there,
Echecrates asks. And did he suffer?
You say you once wounded a deer and chased it
into an aspen grove like this one. The air
between the trunks wavered and seemed to fill
with a hundred deers' dark eyes. Maybe each one
of us could bring an analogy that would suffice.

Days lost to us as in a fog, half our closets unworn,
time not a progression but a lake too easy
to drown in. Bodies, already ghost-like, open as glass.

SEE THROUGH

Her rooms empty slowly, like wavelets
discarding shell and ovoid stones, her back closets
saved for last, silks and sandals. Can she still see
the moon? Does it look the same as from here,
fragmented and silvered with emotions? I cling
to her last words as if they imparted more meaning
just because there will be no more. *Impartire.*
To share, to divide among us. "Hold yourself straight,
little goat," said her dying mother to Virginia Woolf.
"You've got to stop this," said mine about
my sobbing. As we get older, the body speaks louder,
through mitochondria, ancestral genes. Whereas,
when young, *I* was all self. We get used to the change
in hours, less or additional moisture in air,
how so much will become indescribable. Who offers
a tutorial on wind patterns? How to understand
the tides? What watershed do we live near?
Where does it drain? Where did she go when she died?
See through, a phrase we use most often as adjective,
not act—dresses, sleeves, veils, and curtains,
the window of an envelope behind which we place
an address. The minutes we push off into the softness
called sleep before the final folding over of events.
Woolf wrote of the vibrancy she saw in colors
after her mother's death: the glass dome at Paddington
that at sunset glowed red, "as if something were
becoming visible without any effort." Light leaking

from under the door of a crowded room at night.
Or my mother's journals, written when she was my age,
sixty-five, paper so thin the ink kept bleeding through.

II. THE STONE COTTAGE

THE STONE COTTAGE

1.

In the early morning,
straw-glow through the uneven weave of the shades,
and the day
       entering as a crease beneath them.

No flycatchers on the railing
or wood warblers feeding off larvae in the willow trees
       as in the past—
a real place now reassigned as recurring dream.

Here is the story, a rhyme of sorts.
After forty years, I have returned to the village
I first came to as a young adult,
       the same gold rush storefronts still shuttered.

The years go by and my consciousness
       travels with them, dying out as the wind does,
nested in the swaying tree,
then entering an old dispensation with clearer eyes.

Smoke rises from the chimneys, bitter.
Two streams drain into a river clogged with stones and ice.
Half ghost town and half bohemian existence—
       by which I mean where did that girl go?

And am I bound to her?
Indigo, the tiny blue-violet bead of dusk in these mountains
     might be what first drew me here.
But what chain of grandmothers? What invisible church?

2.

I fear the villagers, with their upper hand, are dangerous
to me and those I love.
      They kick over our campaign signs in the snow.

If it is true that history proves that only pessimists survive,
      those who gauge the tipping point,
the turning of the tides, I am calling it far from the shore.

Moonlight on raspberry canes
in a shared backyard, mulch and burlap on roots of cherry
      and pear—this is no country for old women

who are unprepared.
      (Do you really think that I, a woman, am alone here?)
So, with our green houses, while earth starts to catch fire,

so with their active shooter curriculum.
We are revisiting the temples we built when we were young,
      choosing which gods and allies will fill them.

3.

(Stone Cottage, Sussex 1913–1916)

They spent their evenings fencing
      while the war raged on. They called themselves

the Order of the Brothers Minor,
      Yeats chanting his rhymes as he created them,

Pound studying on another floor, each maneuvering
      for the better position.

There, as here, women explored the wilderness—
      a queer lake in the forest—with wonderful-coloured trees,

Dorothy wrote. *It is a weird place—and possibly faerie.*
      Symbolism, in its profounder sense,

Pound explained to his future wife, suggesting grimoires
      of western magic, *The Comte de Gabalis,*

but neglecting the persecution of the witches,
      their reincarnating souls, the traumatic memories

and latent powers they bring here with them. Here, as there,
      the stone cottage I live in

was once a boarding house. Next door was the brothel,
    a row of eight tiny rooms upstairs,

parlor below with its wainscoting and Victorian ceiling.
    Hope Street. Silver Street. Quartz Street.

There as here, men digging desperately in the dirt for gold.
    In caves nearby are pictographs,

evidence of an ancient initiatory culture. Ochre sunbursts,
    handprints, arrows pointing to

the vestibular—deep cracks in the rock surface from which
    antlered and feathered spirits stumble out.

But what were Pound and Yeats searching for
    the three winters they roomed together in Sussex?

What kind of inheritance? *"Pretty green bank" began the half-lost
    poem*, lines Pound copied into his own canto

from notes written by an English alchemist who claimed
    he saw a goddess, *whose foot was leaflike*, whose sleeves

were purple, and who promised a path to holy wisdom,
    perhaps a small stream lined with aspen

like this one, water pooling atop the ice,
    though nothing is lit quite like our metallic grasses.

4.

and the place is full of spirits
Not lemures, not dark and shadowy ghosts,
But the ancient living, wood-white,
Smooth as the inner bark, and firm of aspect

—EZRA POUND

I see their tracks roping loosely in the bottoms, amidst the aspen, most animal of all trees—long-necked, black-spotted, inarticulate without leaves. An anticipatory dream haunts their trunks, humming its water theme, a blood rushing to the crown and elevated through the cells. Of tracks, the deer's glass slipper. The rabbit's keyhole. Miniature railroad ties imprinted by voles. So many presences made visible now because of the snow though bird-abandoned is the sky and thus windowless. What kind of human could we be if we let the cold compress us? Not becoming wind but allowing what it says as it pours in, stripping us of weakened promise and ambition. If one moves to a ghost town, what can one do but converse with ghosts? Whose driveways lead nowhere. Who gaze down on me from the slopes, then slowly turn and disappear inside their houses. Hours pass, rummaging above me like the clouds. The fact is, consciousness matters; matter knows it, a tightly stretched drum. It acknowledges me, an aging woman attempting a last run, though it is sometimes hard for me to find the forest for the damaged fields.

5.

*there as here we do not always know all that is in our
memory*
—WILLIAM BUTLER YEATS

A woman stands atop the flat roof of her trailer house
with a shovel, overlarge boots unlaced.
　　　I wave, but she stares past me into the blizzard.

Past the rundown houses, free of their past inhabitants,
　　　a small cabin with a smokeless chimney,
Gods Grace scrawled on a placard nailed to the fence.

Just when was America great the indigenous people ask,
who come to her in her dreams,
　　　those among the earth's first spiritual adepts.

Do I believe my presence is a spell only the snowfall
　　　can soften? Should my words then
include *to mend*, that ancient orbit of needle and thread?

Should it begin with the phrase *continuing-to-tell-the-story*—
　　　a narrative that is attached to every land?
(Always an under-song of missing and murdered people.)

There were once those who used to see things, hear things,
　　　to whom strange things used to come—
a ghost horse in the mountains, lighted ships far out at sea—

what to do when no one sees them, when nothing sounds?
The woman stares past
        the underfed horses, the menacing front yard dogs,

the foster twins who trade her goose eggs for oxycontin,
the suicide's half-finished barn.
        Who can tell who is really here and who has gone?

6.

in the dark
        ignition of the propane
in the fireplace below
waking us when it flares heat climbing the loft
        frost on the dormer
like summer camp inside the pine ceiling boards low
        Orion in the south by now
and you and I not an old man and wife in winter

though how long has it been
        since we allowed the celestial to surprise us
it happens to everyone I mean loss of our power
        the young have new crises
causes we need them the country taken over by thugs
hush you say
        the night sky is making overtures
blood moon green comet eclipse a rain of falling stars

you for whom I have moved here
        my friend my lover my companion in order
to build a life together
        among others of our kind
I uprooted myself from my solitude will it survive this
        for me
you have crossed a threshold
        carefully crafted and the singleness it defined

as a child my mother always began weeping
           when she entered the spiritualist church the walls
separating her from the dead
                    the medium said were too thin
the animals of my mother's wilderness
                         were wilder than our animals
the men of my mother's adolescence were
                                   far worse than these men

we draw our circles small on purpose
                    to protect the life in question
even the gunman last March skulking down the creek side
           across from where we were splitting wood
was looking for something else to hate
                                        to live for
                    not all is mythic not all is against us
the preacher who wanted to save us now calls for our help

occultists say there are profound consequences
for the persecution by the dominant religious authorities
           of the marginalized the visionaries
the initiates
           and to refuse to correct the imbalances that result
from these errors
                    is insanity a departure from reason
           mine shafts cratered earth slag in our waterways

poor country village with nothing to offer we keep offering
           walking these hills between the armed
and the violently employed
                         what if we reconvened the coven

the cauldron the seance if
we were who they must come to for banishment for healing
decked out in their nationalistic ardor
but louder the spells the mirrors the bridge the mediation

because I was born in winter
my touchstone is starlight you were born
in summer and your mentor is the sun
your first thoughts were of your missing twin
I was ill-taken from my mother
if we don't achieve the world that our lives call for
or the changes it demands
we can still forge this common thread a shared hermitage

7. Figments: a spell

Cloud-shapes and ice-forms and names of local winds,
the chickadees who remain our friends
because we have created a haven inside us for them

Kin of the mountain, its peculiar resounding call
as if through empty subterranean halls,
the flicker of torchlight spreading across the walls

Figment or fragment, thought come alive in front of me,
the village bells quieting as the snow falls thickly
onto paths I have shoveled, onto boughs of the tree

The meeting of a consciousness and a particular place:
surely we cannot expect the earth to embrace us
if we don't offer our hands, if we don't turn and face it

I throw rocks, aiming to hit close to the river's edge
as the black herds stampede under the frozen ledge—
water trying to break through, trying to hear what is said

Wind that comes at night squeezing through the cracks,
wind brief and muscular, wind that is fat
and bites at noon, drifts that reveal the north wind's track

You who are always looking for colors in snowfield glitter,
natural yet ornamental, pink or mint or
azure, its silver leaf embossed with salt, chimes, and crystal,

pay close attention to where you are now, note that
everything will change tomorrow, including your motives,
the seasons, the currents, the meteors exploding,

and what floated before aquifers, their fragile bones piling
into seabed, rock shelves, perforated linings,
an origin like lace—full of holes—a myth of water filling

I could believe in a god like that—comprehensible—
like the overlong, loose sleeves of sky, three-dimensional,
billowing with ghost pavilions, but reachable, sensing us

III. THE PATH OF MELTING ICE

More and more, the pressing human dilemma:
how to walk a clean path between obscenities.
—ALI SMITH

THE LUPINE PATH

Ashes of roses is a color, not a sentiment.
The lupine hold out their deeply divided hands.
Collectively, without scent.
Stream-like now, in their extremes of happiness.

Lupine, of the same family as the wisteria
I once saw draped over horse-drawn carriages
in a bewilderingly silent parade.
Powdered faces of the Japanese expressionless.

Like any metaphor, the lupine path is a window,
not a mirror. The image and its meditative
counterpart. Its hidden sound.
Faceted like a bird with the breath of pine in it.

Or the lace bodice of my grandmother's
dress-up dress, her everyday printed with violets—
walking here without her, insular
as a child, my ankles are brushed as if by moths.

The soul composed of small atoms produces
small dream stations, a poet writes.
A flower corridor, perhaps a processional.
The word *branch* does not carry with it the leaves.

In my case, the path was narrow, a tunnel
through the thick stands, which offered no views

of the corresponding mountains.
Summer creek bed so shallow I crossed on stones.

When you get to the end of something,
I have heard, turn around before going forward.
Where I have been: the death of my mother,
which I attended, and a friend's, her beautiful

childlike singing. You can be a meadowlark
breaking in my ears.
When I gained the skill of anticipatory weeping.
When my mouth, as if stuffed with silken rags.

CLIFF LAKE

A flock of blackbirds disappears into the surface of sky.
We're still here, on the other side of the fading.
A turbulent presence. A waterfall within lake water that is calm.

The animals who have come before us,
and those who will come long after we are gone—
if I lose my hearing, all that will be preserved is their sound.

I read a poet once who imagined the rustle of Turkish silk,
which she heard in years past, had migrated into her poetry.

Down one arm, hundreds of rainbow trout,
their swerve seen through the sun-yellow clarity of the water.

Our gifts—we cannot will them into view. They awake
like an eye wakes to the wave-shape of light.
Down the second arm, which is the longest, are the swans.

Everything often is metaphor, the wonder of a lead
amid the rushes where the duck and her ducklings go to hide.
But why be impatient for its opening?

We watch as two swans lift from the lake, creating four
shapes, perfectly replicate. Surely grace, that not one collides.

It seems we can at any given moment be witness,
to the osprey chick, for instance, flapping its tall wings, who
suddenly finds itself careening over the forest.

Most birds once they've fledged never return to the nest.
To never. To do never. What courage
must that take. And why must everything still be about us?

THE DOCTRINE OF SIGNATURES

Given my disposition, I will always be
circuitous, precocious, an Embellisher.
— LUCIE BROCK-BROIDO

Given my character, I will always be
the fir out my window—slow to act, to make decisions.

Given my disposition, I will live my life in one place,
not trembling like the aspen, but swaying
like the heavy spruce, troubled by forces larger than me—

the wind, the rains, the sun. Do you know what radiant
means, I asked the pretty child at the party
who was not aware of the word that she was wearing.

When you come, the beginning of a letter I wish to write,
when you come, this summer, when you stay with me.

Given my disposition, I will always be retractable,
with my father's long hands and feet.
If I want, glittered and posturing. If I don't, like the willow,

slouching. Given my temperament, I can be found
where the wood orchid spreads, under an awning of pines.
In the pale hour, before dawn, which belongs to deer.

Böhme believed that God marked each object with a sign
so that humans would know which ones could cure.
Walnut, for brain injuries, headaches. Rosehip, for snot

and tears. Bone-knit, the common name of comfrey.
If form is of the essence, what do the magicians have to say?
If you know, keep silent and say nothing to the scoffers.

To employ the doctrine of signatures, you must identify
the shape of your distress. The shape for grief—
a charred tree. A broken wing. Or maybe not the shape

of the disease, but its location. Where fear might be found.
The nerves. A trembling mycorrhizal web. Given
my disposition, in old age, I will be susceptible as the wind.

THE PRICKLY PEAR PATH

Some years we don't see the bobolinks
in the hayfields. In spring, the bluebird migrations
     may be spare.
Someday, if we are lucky, we will fan out across
     identical miles of sage and find
your walking stick exactly where you forgot it.

We thirst and the earth offers water.
We are born with a taste for the planet's food.
Out of thorniness, out of dust and flat endurance,
     a fragility amidst harshness,
prickly pear blossoms ripping open in the heat.

It is patriarchy that makes men violent,
not an inherent violence in themselves, Butler writes.
If we dress boys as flowers, will it gentle them?

My mother admonished me for using the word *hate*.
I thought she simply meant to not get angry.
     I didn't understand how the strength
of its wind makes it impossible to feel anything else.

I always wanted to be a flower, but an invisible one,
     while you wished to be a pink cloud,
light-hearted at the core. Dear Earth,
I hope you survive us. It's luxurious to sleep with you.

A lonely blue spiral that holds us close in its arms,
　　　　how long will weather be bearable?

My lifetime or yours? The app that shows the young
　　　　what they will look like in old age
presumes they need to know now that it will happen.

The fact is we *do* live here. With the fairies.
I have watched them climb down,
　　　　warblers, ambassadors from distant boughs,
bathed now in dappled sun and heightened rain.

We borrow from Earth all the metaphors we will need.
Out of loveliness, violence. Out of violence,
　　　　these yellow blooms.
Dead End, which the road sign says under the rainbow.

SELF PORTRAIT AS APPARITION

Winter before dawn. I emerge from the pines.
Not the highway light we drive through,
not midday's omniscient beam, but the half-shuttered
canyon I loved so well this time of year.
Like coming upon an emptied house of one deceased.

The front door has shrunken. No need for a key.
The white plaster walls are smooth and cold as the bark
of aspen, the ceiling splitting at its seams.
No fire blazes, as it once had, no running water
or kettle steam. Wind taps its fingers against the glass.

I go to the windows—something was always there—
move to the treetops, searching
for solitaires, the black-capped chickadees, the birds
who stay. Gone forever: my favorite places,
years on my grandparents' farm. Even my childhood

houses are fading, my parents' punched-in doors.
Necessary, but now totally replaceable. Did I betray
my life by leaving it? Red wool blankets once covered
this stripped bed. A lover slept sometimes
next to me. We entered each morning quiet as the dust.

I am amazed at how far I traveled, by how frugal I lived.
A wooden table in the living room,
a few paintings by friends. Shelter: I have never needed

very much. The sun touches the pine boughs
as if with kindness, and the new snow shimmers down.

Who am I if I am voiceless? Voiceless, I am too aware
of my appearance—unprotected, genderless,
and bare as a small girl. I move through the translucent
corridors, as the fish do, keeping to their lanes.
If you get too close, I will dissolve, along with my words.

Yet perhaps you have eyes only for the human.
Perhaps the two grouse, like me, are ghosts, clambering
up the flimsy limbs, too heavy for their perch,
while a third one makes its clumsy way across the snow.
Perhaps you see the world without believing I am in it.

THE ASPEN PATH

The aspen leaves have fledged and so
        are distant, having traveled
into their exterior summer lives,
        preoccupied now with living, not dreaming.
A loss of intimate relation.
Though breezes move toward me with softer hands.

Why can't I approach my own growth
        with such undivided intentions?
Without new teachers, I revisit
        the rituals, a star I make room for
        in a small asymmetrical window,
pussy willow soaking its roots in an earthenware cup.

The phases come. The trunks are timeless.
As if the moon were shining on them through the day.
        All light enters us
        without permission.
The logic is unanswerable: aging is the body's crime.
        I stand under trees as if under their influence.

Water everywhere to read this season.
        See, it has swallowed the highest stone.
The rainbow-lipped branches
        in the gradual thaumaturgy of spring rain—
we each have an instrument.
        It wakes the younger ones first,

the rest reluctant to start again with tarnished horns.
        Aging: my solstice,
                I didn't notice the turn.
Was the dawn different when I was seven years old
than it will be when I am seventy?
        As if sisters. As if one of them is gone.

Sixty hours before the asteroid hit,
they say, it appeared like a star, swimming ever faster
        toward us.
                Ninety-nine percent of life died.
Seventy-five percent of species went extinct.
        Mammals, even plants, must have felt uneasy.

If there is such a story, larger than our memories
        of earth, there must be an equally large story
of what is not life.
        If there is a process or do all processes stop.
It is difficult to imagine *us* in the past—
maybe why my grandmother's eyes were always watering.

A friend said
    she gets more beautiful all the time about his friend
who is dead. As she passes, does she shed
her deterioration?
    Just as I wanted to bring an aspen into my room,
to duplicate it in paint, nothing common left for very long.

THE CHOKECHERRY PATH

Miraculously healed, the vet said, of all but old age,
your cat dozes in shade under the boughs.
This fruit, mostly pit, so I have to pick for hours,
doors opening in the distance, a neighbor
practicing his trombone, the same outdated tune
for thirty years. Back at home,
bald-faced hornets in the raspberries, infiltrating
the last of the season's spoils,
clinging sugar-drunk, territorial, even unto dusk.
It has been a summer of night blooms, caddis flies
raining, creating a thick smear.
I had to stop at a gas station to scrub them off.
This heat, does it birth them?
As Bishop said, maybe we should stay where we are,
but what if here is so drastically altered?
Last week, I watched a woman in a kayak pull away
from land, causing her little dog to go crazy.
It leaped into the water though she wasn't sure
it could swim, fast, before it knew what it was doing.
That image, an archetype surely—
people on board waving as a ship backs from the pier,
then panic as those left behind grow smaller.
"Farewell! Farewell!!" they wave more desperately.
Worse, when it happens quickly,
for those who never get to say goodbye, though maybe
we should say it as often as we say hello.
You made one mistake and are on crutches
for months, your ability to walk irreparably damaged.

The hornets are insults, as well as insects
so dangerous that I gave up: raspberries, a summer
evening in the yard. I have made enough jam,
enough to share. Your chokecherries
I will boil into dark purple syrup. The jars
we will split, a bargain that we have waged as friends.

THE BITTERROOT PATH

It blooms without precedent
or prudence,
outside laws leaflessly, appears unannounced
in the dust, radiant
amid the already worn, the earth-burnt.

If we live in mythic times
the American bitterroot could be a signet,
a crest
of bleached out rose,
pinpointing. An ancient source, ignored.

Read the headlines.
Scientists are worried about our health
in an increasingly noisy world.
I used to be so certain my solitude
would be disturbed I cried in anticipation of it.

When were we most quiet? Listening
to the speech of herbs.
I mean, an inner quiet—
coming from not being able to control anything.
Isn't that what flowering does?

To become such a spiritual delicacy.
A vision wavering in front of us, then failing
in the heat.
Me, shrinking back to what I was as a girl,

ashamed of it, smelling of menses.
Rebirthing themselves in string-like stems,
the pink bells of the buds barely lift
above the ground.
We are drawn to the bright upper cadences—
while the bitter roots hide underneath.

OVERLAY

She starts with a map. In the lower
right corner, there should be a compass rose,
but how to orient in the accumulation
of such loss?

                    Plotted and pieced,
the green might have sheltered them
in forests of spruce and pine,
blue square of willow copse by the waterway,

goldenrod signifying the empty, endless miles—
instead the colors declare how
the earth is owned.
                    Atop the official grid,

she begins to superimpose her own designs.
Here, a remnant of red
silk-velvet, a best-dress laid upon the ground,
stitched with rows of trade beads and cowries.

If we could only read the floral patterns she has
sewn around it, the Salish, fabric leaves,
bitterroot like a birthmark,
mountain bluebell, the stems and herbal seams,

if we could enter the beaded circles
that mark where each woman at last was seen—

beside which Grief sits,
reaching her arm far as possible down the well.

Every culture seems to have a story
about a daughter disappearing into earth or sky.
The black bear overtakes her, a snake
bites her, a white swan slowly spreads his wings.

In the end, it is always said to be her fault—
she was drinking, she was hitchhiking, she was too beautiful,
she was with a man. She is dragged
to the underworld or sent to live with the stars.

In the worst places, the circles cluster
like a ring toss. Everywhere, the highways expand,
their yellow lines the danger zones the women
crossed in common.

                              In truth,
the map still begs for their return. I stood outside
the capitol and watched a mother cry.
Wind through her hair enough to break my heart.

SPARROW POND

I had thought the pond was named not for what is there, but for
what lies along the path. Whether I call out for bear, or not, the
sparrows spill. Impossible to count them. They appear so much
the same. The blink of a raindrop. A moment they fly into just
as it seals itself off. Every description begins with other species
the bird resembles: the chipping and vesper, the Brewer's and
song, subverting my pleasure in identification. *Of being numerous*,
George Oppen wrote, the question at the heart. When you reach
a certain age, don't you become bored with your own story,
wishing for a fresh translation, a new plot? In the wetlands, every
swallow is common and starred. Two trumpeter swans float so
close that they become almost one, their white necks more floral
than animal. If we care only about the human, if our binoculars
are focused there—our perspective will be hopelessly diagnostic.
I have found myself guilty. How could I not as time unfolds,
though I have never believed in our conventions of it, as if time
were orderly, spread out like a letter by a people who no longer
write, one unable to reference death in its scroll. When I learned
that the pond was named after a man, not the bird, not the path,
it didn't change my poem at all.

THE GLITTER PATH

I have to reach out farther in winter
to bring the smell of stars in: menthol and metallic
like sagebrush, remonstrative, a tang.
Green-white, opalescent with an under-layer of changing blue,
H.D. wrote, but she, too, had trouble naming
their fragrance. *Invent it,* her interior
patron advised. Ice flannels over the soft earth
but textures the freezing river: candle ice,
frost roses, acicular crystals. I can't tell if the ice
where the water slides is adding
to its store at noon or is slowly being eaten away.
In last night's dream, your dead brother
helps the family pick up garbage along the road,
but he grows tired, lies down, turns invisible.
What is new, what is new, the chickadee sings
in the underbush, who lives only three to five years.
Who is in your cast? Your evidentiary stars?
We walk through the winter pines, wind stirring up
snow from their boughs, reminding you
that you once took your mother to Cirque du Soleil
—those silvery costumes, the toss of
shimmering rings—a world apart, light years ago.
We will all become invisible, but have we ever shone?
A galaxy. A milky snowpath. Thousands of
colored sparks, glitter in the tracks we leave behind.

THE PATH OF MELTING ICE

We come from nothing we can remember,
and travel toward a place we know nothing about,
the margins of our lives closed to us.
Like a block of ice in a sea of ice breaking apart.
As it is, we lower ourselves to the next
eschatological landing. As it is, we step barefoot
over our own stones. At midnight,
two large mule deer strut down the village road
and stand at my gate, considering its height.
Under a street lamp, a few hours of their reign.
The creek runs under a lambswool blanket.
The huge gray owl on the path is also a tree.
From the threadbare places where the creek opens,
its sound reaches my ears. It wears the scent
of pine. It dresses in disarray. If it is true that
our relationships are patterned after archetypes,
who then is earth to me? Not wife, certainly
not husband. Because I disavowed the supremacy
of my father, I never worshiped the male gods,
the arsenals in their increasingly violent displays.
Remember, when we were first together,
how you would make the bed while I brewed tea,
arranging my pajamas as if I were still
underneath them, each day a different pose,
a scarecrow atop the blankets that made us laugh?
We are moving into war again, the continents
on fire, our neighbors turning swiftly aggressive.
Strange to think we inhabit these bodies only once.
I wish I could express all they have meant to me.

IV. SLEEP PRACTICE

My coming, my going—
Two simple happenings
That got entangled.

—KOZAN ICHIKYO

THE FERN PATH

Green blossoms of the water host, the splayed
riparian fronds—four feet wide and still
dripping from the all-day rain. But why describe
what is still new to me, as the poet Stéphane
Mallarmé asked, instead of searching for the flower
absent from all earthly bouquets. Oyster light,
islanders call it when sun barely leaks through clouds.
Who taught me what is hidden is more valuable?
Quiet is different than silence, the latter more potent,
more mature. Quiet is self-conscious, shallow,
in making others bend to hear you, an aesthetic choice,
as in the quiet of these mixed diurnal tides,
which happen twice a day but not in regular patterns.
What silence means: an unaccountable caesura,
as in no new deaths were recorded in the last week.
It is silence that subtracts from the great harbor
the boats. It is not silence without my lost ones in it.
As if a cloth were bunched and dipped in housepaint,
flecked with silver and moss, then pressed against
the trunks, the cedars seem ceremonially prepared.
Underneath are plants that live faintly, like ground mist,
and those anchored so deep they don't sway,
those that line up along the rivulets, the single runners.
Without language, how do they reach each other?
I lose the way only once, not recognizing the broken
limbs, the identical black snags stuffed with duff,
or stumps cloaked with extravagant emerald fringe.
The dead—there are so many—often take the same pose,

on their backs, in obeisance to the exuberant lichen.
They leave the world like this, spilling over its boundaries,
awash. So much oxygen I find it difficult to breathe.

SLEEP PRACTICE

Brown, I say in sleep practice and the tiny birds
with upturned tails appear. I add the round
brown vole slowly dragging its lame back leg. Winter
wren. A ruby-crowned kinglet. One by one,
I nestle them atop my head, behind an ear, the bushtit
in a palm held at my stomach. I am a stall,
a manger, words I borrow from the farm, my wish
to become for them a place to shelter. To stall is
to interrupt, to stop a forward movement or thought.
Fighting the mind, who or what is its opponent?
I am trying to eliminate speech that lacks confidence—
maybe, kind of, as if. I want to practice faith,
not belief, faith in the day brought back to me,
faith that the vole will find food if only it ventures out
from under snow to scavenge. To return to them
is my assignment. Yellow, I say, and the alder catkins
by the pond begin to dangle. Purple, the dark bog
I couldn't walk through, a stench of bergamot and rot.
White lichen pasted on the trunks of vine maple.
In the Ondaatje novel I am reading, the nun
blown off the bridge in a storm becomes an actress,
sheds her robe, and grows her hair. The day path
is erratic and elbowed like the flight of gulls.
The nun then chooses Alice Gull for her new name.

SLEEPING WITH THE CEDARS

Smaller than hours and waves, I lie
in their shade. Daubed with their paste. A form
of peace in the island green of mourning.

When I graduate, my mother used to say,
one of our little jokes. To graduate, a step-by-
step affair. The silence is like a Bronze

Age bell tolling. Announcing her death, which
I know of already, or declaring a new
phase. In order for the community to gather.

In the Egyptian Book of the Dead,
Osiris waits in the dark to burst forth, hitting air
as a swallow, a falcon, a craftsman, a snake,

a lotus, but never a tree. My mother complained
that I dress like a widow, my hair like bark
or ash and that I intentionally neglect to brush it.

It is instead the shyness of those most favored
that makes me hide, like pigment blended
with water and spread across the surface of a sky

made to wrinkle and absorb it. Wake me,
let me walk again, the dead plead in the Egyptian
hymns. As my mother did when she was alive.

Lift your eyes. Can you find the one branch
wavering in the Forest of No Wind?
Strong emotion must leave its trace, the writers say.

The painters know, within the trunks of cedar,
there are many carved wooden rooms,
sunlight pouring forth from doors they left ajar.

SLEEPING WITH THE EAGLES

The sea, the ever-recommensing sea.
—PAUL VALÉRY

It's the talons, not the beak, you should be afraid of.
Eagles can catch a goose in flight. The trick
is to stand as still as you can, your heart pounding
loud, tireless as the surf where you first saw them,
facing into the rain, fishing the estuaries.
How you begin and end your days should be filled
with import, as from a foreign or external force.
All the while, while you live far from it, the ocean lives,
its wingspan enormous, its turbulence
beaked, as if it were gripped by something monstrous
and shaken hard. In order to remember anything,
you must return to the place. Silver-blue, sea salt,
the chill before the event, how you picked up
and discarded the egg-shaped stones that rolled in,
the flat black saucers you took home to line your paths.
You don't want trouble. You just want to know
that you're okay. You have your daily experience,
and then what in changing changes you: this pleroma
of vegetation, holly, blackberry, and fern. Cedar
bark cast in the greenest impasto. The moon.
The sea, the ever-recommencing sea. You had hoped
living near water would make you kinder. The Chinese
thought it would make one wise. Still, there are
encounters that are harder to register. A line of young
women donned their masks as you, an older woman,

stepped aside, turned their backs to you on the trail even
as they greeted you. What makes a heart beat faster?
Epinephrine, an ice skid, sudden rising of ocean waves.
Two eagles on the floating dock at the edge of sleep.
Although it is best to take off running like the gulls do,
you invite them, make room for them, guardians and
threat. You don't choose the gods, only those who come.

NOCTURNE

Outside town, past the house of the carpenter,
a house he built with his own hands,
at night, the stream is louder for no witnesses
but the white-tail deer who descend to drink
and the low, unseen creatures who rustle
under leaves that seem to gleam despite the dark.
I have always wanted to live in a second story.
Like many women my age, I do not sleep well.
Pill bottles line my cabinet like little dancers
ready to perform. Nightlights glare like sterile stars.
A solitude watched is a solitude interrupted.
Yet I sometimes wish for those I would be happy
to encounter on these streets, the spring twilight
in no hurry to leave. As if I were granted
an extra hour, an extraneous room, and I found
others there, too, in good moods, like mine,
after drinking. The carpenter, for instance,
how we stood together, four nights before he died,
admiring the hand-hewn logs, the dove-tailed
corners. Yes, I am building a piano, he said.
A door opened and a festive light poured through,
onto me, onto the crowd gathering behind us.

SPARROW HOUSE

No one remembers the hotel being open
or when the second-story window glass fell out.
A fire that smoked the alley-side. The bricks
beginning to dislodge. The mortar loosening.
Overtaken, not infested, but opportune.
Winter afternoons, the nearby lilac fills
with sparrows. The downstairs curtain rod sags,
revealing a laundry room—sinks and shelves
of bedding. Like a diorama of a ghost town
in the midst of the living town, there is nothing
new to learn and no access. For instance,
no one else seems to notice the birds' trespass,
loudest sound around, the metered argument
rising and falling in pitch and volume.
Bald eagles require distance between their nests,
but sparrows board close like we do. They
fan out in good weather, fattening on our seeds,
too small to lend warmth to the plaster walls.
Smooth and cold like the dead body of anything.
Do you have a book in you? I've had many,
but now they've flown, strange valor of aviation.
Generations are born. They seem to have a lot
to say, even as the world grows parsimonious.
The old world, I mean, the old lives, which
go on telling their stories: this is what happened
in the heart of winter, or should we say soul,
the deepest part, the bottom of the well,
if there were still wells, if we still looked into them.

THE SLEEP PATH

The blankets glimmer, coated with my hair,
which falls onto the sleep path like silver leaves.
Will I be as a bare tree, no inspiration to anyone?
A perching place? A snag in air? I am dripping
hair, like letters in Apollinaire's calligramme of rain.
The internet says it can happen with extreme illness
or trauma. I remember my illness, suffered
in quarantine. I remember my mother's last days,
as I ran, panicked, through the burning fields
as the castle crumbled behind me. A woman without
a religious life or rules. In the past, mourners
wore black for a hundred days, shuttered windows,
draped mirrors. No one could sweep or shave.
Today, there is no grave to speak of. No earrings,
nor the yellow dress that we picked out. I came back
from the grief-forest, wishing to be powdered
with rain, to streak my hair with green in solidarity.
But here I am, ashes. As is. Let everyone
have their sadness. Let my mother have hers, too.
How she wept when we told her about the rainbow
because she couldn't get out of bed. Why
is the phrase *nursing our wounds* seen as so pejorative?
The name I go by is what my mother chose for me.
But what to use to secretly *call myself*? Even if
she's no longer here. Even as I am walking toward her.

SPRING SNOW

The pool is quiet and almost still.
We bring and burn what we have been taught to.
The ashes chalk our hands before we toss them.
They hit the light midair then fall, creating
a disturbance. Little storms, clouded with calcium.
Mother. Father. I portion out enough
for each to sink. I imagine they will be gone
by the summer. My own prayer jar is emptying.
As it should be. I don't have time for bones
to become white lilac. For them to bleed into a tree.
Ancestors, who like to see their faces on us—
but I am childless. My most intelligent friends
reluctant to conceive. I often wish for the shallows
when I am being steered toward the depths.
Though it's not a passive life, water positions itself.
Today, clouds move over the mountains in
godlike approach, turn to slow fat flakes the size
of moths. They seem to prefer falling to flying.
Like the water dipper that would rather dip its wings.

SLEEPING WITH THE MOON

At the edge of another winter,
the sky a black tea, flavored with mint
and cream, the moon is in a window
I have to move my head to see,
though its light rubs against my feet,
rough and ceramic. I have only
one door out that leads to another door
that opens onto the middle of town.
A silver apple tree under the street lamps.
I resist the need for parenthesis.
I take the extra steps to reach outside.
Like many women, I have felt
the moon within me, sleeping on
my side, holding the fat of its soft belly
in my hands. Earth wants to help us,
doesn't it? Even so, the moon?
Even as we circle closer to extinction.
Surely, the animals, too, sense this.
Maybe their dreams are filled with stories
of us, as ours always are of them:
the Four Sisters of the Last Forest,
one of whom is named Grief, three men
who go to the moon, leaving footprints
so brief—buried in lunar dust—that
they forever yearn to go back. Or two
old women, having fallen in love,
who head for the mountains with a little
tent. No matter that cold is imminent.

THE WILLOW PATH

Alive inside the shawl of myth and earth,
I come to renew my tithing. I come to the willows,
the slant rhyme of their multi-limbed clatter
in wind, and invite them in to my dreams tonight.
My senses have grown thick, barely registering
the rose thorn, scraping against the barbs
of the wireless, the threatening voices that fill the air.
Why not come here? Why not believe it matters?
My mother has known me the longest.
No other person will ever know me in this way.
Because I live in a loft, I can feel the timbers sway,
a comfort they take from the stars.
If there will really be an event called the rapture,
I hope it takes the others and leaves me a path
that skirts the edge of town to climb the mountain.
Wind boxes my ears, culling the dead, piling up
breakage in the ditches. No war is holy.
What about the 144,000 souls waiting to disappear?
Will they exit the thicket, like these deer do?
The tips of their branches form a single crown,
a membrane breathing open and shut, involuntary
and protective as our eyelids in sleep. Without leaves,
a tree is most exposed and most ignored.
The sky is not moving. Light moves through it
instead to this bed it keeps returning to below clouds.
I have come here for their peace and instructions.

CHIONOPHILES

Those with oversized paws that keep them
from sinking. Those with thick fur, the ermine,
the Arctic hare, those with feathers, tundra swans
and snow geese. Those who vow a practice,
which accumulates over many days, as a seed finds
its way to the surface. Moving nonviolently,
from nowhere that we can see. Where does your
attention lead? What do you go to most willingly?
It is March, nearing the end of it, the sky
pale and clear, exhausted, as if after a long illness.
Love of snow: shoveling the narrow paths
from one threshold to another. Reading poorly
the creatures who step in stitches or run a long dash.
Recognizing only the fox, which drags its tail.
Those who can stand atop where we fall through.
What are the smells that will stay with you,
say, pine needles and wood smoke, what particular
direction, what certain view, where you watch
pine boughs grow heavy and drop their white veils
in sprays that ignite one by one down the slopes.
How facing them you have felt cool and reluctant.
We don't often ask the right questions of each other.
Have you ever had a *supernatural* experience?
What has hurt you the worst? Did nature ever talk
to you, teach you? Who do you miss the most?
If you have one, what is the sound of your prayer?

THE MOTHER TREE

The question the forest researcher was obsessed with
is whether the dying Mother Tree, *facing an uncertain future,*
can transfer her remaining resources to her young.
My face was next to hers on the pillow when my mother
took her last breath. Grief shoots through my body,
from my throat down to my feet. Vascular, when I let myself
remember this. But it is trees I want to write about,
their tangible fungal cords, how they can recognize their kin,
and help accordingly, favoring them with carbon,
nitrogen, and water, and, if they are strong, sharing what is
left with other species. And it is the lesser scaups
that I want to write about, on the shallow, algae-filled river,
how they scurried in front of our canoe because
the young could not yet fly, some tiny as the newest kitten,
all panicking at our approach, a few paddling past us
in the wrong direction. "Gulls are assholes," said my friend,
as we watched them arrive and immediately begin
dive-bombing the ducklings. Such genius, how they huddled,
then dove underwater each time the gulls swooped low,
bobbing up where and when no one expected them.
Later, a biologist tells me gulls will do this until the babies
are so exhausted they give up, floating on the water like,
well, like sitting ducks, that the gull is their primary predator.
My mother said that she hoped, if there was a heaven,
it would be filled with love, quickly clarifying that she meant
without the usual lust and violence. The forest researcher,
diagnosed with breast cancer, hoped to leave something
to her daughters. The scaups always know who goes astray.

SLEEPING WITH THE SWANS

It is the swan's proximity to dream
          that allows the sleep exercise to serve its purpose.
Lullaby, from the Middle English *lullen*,
          to cradle, to lull, to ride the hypnotic lapping
of waves. You have been restless, doubtful,
          but you also know enough to wait it out.
You can have days like this, weeks, *in the circle of artist time,*
          when you waddle through transformation,
the shame of swans. You can't reach their world directly.
          Your steps suck into the moat of mud.
What if everyone were given refuge, if there were habitat
          set aside, no gunfire, no lack of water,
no poisonous food or air, where, without interruption,
          we could thrive? And why not atonement
for outright theft? The French for swan is a homonym for
          sign. The *cygne* on the wound,
René Char wrote, a hurt on the surface anyone can see.
          Why we could use a white wing folded over it.
Trumpeters, for instance, not tundras or mutes, beaks painted
          black and glossy for a parade. Lore has it, they live
by metaphor, signatories of grace, a habit you have fallen
          out of the habit of. Imperturbable—
it is not so much beauty as their apparent ease, sailing
          across the pond, pushed by a gentle breeze,
no lice, no lead, no collisions with glass or planes, how they
          don't smell sour and grassy like other birds do.
Though some flaws are biological. Heavy, they need

a long run to lift off, which requires a precise weighing
of each threat. It is lift that you, too, are after, and after it,
the calm. But what to do about the wounded swans?

REPRIEVE

Watching it move up the valley in its plentitude
between the mountains and me, the rain
soaking into each particle of soil, glistening
on the tip of each leaf, like the old myth
of a god who sees our every thought and deed—
impossible, but why not, if rain can do this?
Rain: one thing and a billion things. Listen as it
ebbs and pounds, sheets of rain blown
in a breathing pattern. I put on my bright blue
raincoat. I walk in my neighbor's door.
"How beautiful," she exclaims at the sight of me,
who, from inside her dementia, must be huge
and shining like the first balloon an infant sees,
one of those days that stays in your heart.
The morning broke without the sound of barking.
As in the bombs stopped falling. A migraine
cleared. My neighbor's words rose to the surface,
this time, the right ones. We all know miracles
don't last. That's why we call them a reprieve,
whether we mean *last* as in the last kiss,
last as in to endure, or *last* as in one end of a race.
I never thought that my final years would be
spent fighting so many threats, including the threat
that these are earth's final years, too. Hope
is necessary, I understand, even if unreasonable,
although hope is not exactly a reprieve. Listen.
The rain's arrival sounds less like crying than gliding
into shore. Minor, short-lived, but still a pardon.

SLEEPING WITH THE DEER

I once had a student who would vow
to speak no words for a week,
notifying me ahead of class by email.
I called her the deer person—
curious, shy. I somehow understood
she still read the assignments carefully.

Buoyancy, that's something we haven't felt
for a while. Wisdom, the Zen monks say,
is a ready mind. Mastery: if we
could detach ourselves from individuality
and yet retain a deeply specific voice.
An owl becoming the village voice at night.

Flank against flank, the friendlier mule deer
gather, then the skittish white tail.
Only the does can slip under the heavy lid
of wakefulness. The bucks bed alone,
backed against rocks or the trunks of trees.
They huff as they settle, non-conversant.

As if I were helping someone carry
a large, non-ambulatory child, my past
has turned awkward and untenable.
I use packets of flower seeds to bookmark
my place through the winters.
Even the person with two parents is gone.

Biologists say that the deer are synanthropic.
As if this weren't their world, too. I read
the news on my phone, and my mind fills.
A thought, like a coat snagged on barbed wire
because I didn't duck low enough to clear it—
the deer will still be here to suffer with us.

THE VALLEY

Assume they are here. In the mist. In morningtide.
Eventide. In exchange of their day for ours, the one with shadows.
It seems wrong to disturb them in their transition
from grazing to pause, the climb from threshold to higher elevation.
Two white-tailed deer are kneeling as they pass under
a barbed wire fence. Like meeting quietude, their bodies perfectly
coordinate. I hear the clack of cranes in the distance,
their wooden rattles accompanying their far-fetched dance.
I am not yet too old that I can't hear the geese flying above me.
Like something out of a myth, one we might refer to
in speaking of a former world, the one before the fires, the flash
floods, the record-breaking heat. They have shown me
their sacred places, a pool pure enough to drink, a sparrow-rimmed
pond, clogged with sea grass, where the white-faced ibis
hunts the mud, its beak a scythe, its feathers darkly iridescent.
My mother sometimes walks with me here, a little slower
for the cane. Her touch is faint—a fault of mine—under-imagined.
One must live in a place a long time to notice the corner
of a boulder, smoothed into a curve by buffalo rubbing against it
for hundreds of years. The valley hasn't opened up to me
fully, but again, it hasn't closed. As the deer are a kind of kindness.
As the moose are good at dares. As the understory fills the air
with scarlet baneberry and goldenrod. I try again to see
my mother passing into the ground-cloud ahead. Cool and moist,
it presses against her skin. She, too, watches, as it separates,
and the mist begins to lift, granting half a portion to sky, a *godsend*,
and half to earth, what might be called a *godreturn*. Where
the eared grebes, breeding, display their ridiculously long, gold-
powdered tufts. Where the deer were once here, in willow sanctums.

NOTES

BIRTH PLACE: "Repressing haste, as too unholy." John Keats. *The Fall of Hyperion.*

THE STONE COTTAGE: "a queer lake in the forest—with wonderful-coloured trees. It is a weird place—and possibly faerie." qtd. in James Longenbach. *Stone Cottage: Pound, Yeats, and Modernism.* "'Pretty green bank' began the half-lost poem." Longenbach.

"and the place is full of spirits / Not lemures, not dark and shadowy ghosts, / But the ancient living, wood-white, / Smooth as the inner bark, and firm of aspect." Ezra Pound. "Three Cantos," qtd. in James Logenbach. Modernist Poetics of History: Pound, Eliot, and the Sense of the Past.

"there as here we do not always know all that is in our memory, but at need angelic spirits . . . act upon us there as here, widening and deepening the consciousness at will." William Butler Yeats. "Swedenborg, Mediums, and the Desolate Places," in Visions and Beliefs in the West of Ireland by Lady Gregory.

THE LUPINE PATH: "The soul composed of very small atoms produces small dream-stations." Ewa Chrusciel. *Contraband of Hoopoe.*

THE DOCTRINE OF SIGNATURES: "Given my disposition, I will always be / circuitous, precocious, an Embellisher." Lucie Brock-Broido. *A Hunger.*

OVERLAY: The poem is in response to an artwork by Lakota artist Molly Murphy Adams entitled *Epicenter and Impact* (in the collection of the Missoula Art Museum).

THE GLITTER PATH: "green-white, opalescent / with an under-layer of changing blue." H.D. *Trilogy*.

SLEEPING WITH THE CEDARS: "strong emotion must leave a trace." Virginia Woolf. *Moments of Being*.

THE MOTHER TREE: "facing an uncertain future". Suzanne Simard. *Searching for the Mother Tree: Discovering the Wisdom of the Forest*.

SLEEPING WITH THE SWANS: "in the circle of Artist time." René Char. "From Moment to Moment," *Selected Poems*, eds. Mary Ann Caws and Tina Jolas.

OWL NEST is for Terri and Jeff Claasen. THE CHOKECHERRY PATH is for Trinka Michalson. AFTER THE VACCINE is for Terry Minow. SELF-PORTRAIT AS APPARITION is for Tenzin Phuntsog.

ACKNOWLEDGMENTS

Grateful acknowledgment to the editors of the following journals, in which some of these poems first appeared:

About Place Journal: "Sleeping with the Deer"
Basalt: "Overlay"
Colorado Review: "Nocturne"
Cutbank: "The Bitterroot Path" and "The River Path"
Denver Quarterly: "The Valley"
The Gettysburg Review: "The Prickly Pear Path" and "The Lupine Path"
High Desert Journal: "Glass Vocabulary," "The Snow Geese Path," and "Self Portrait as Apparition"
Pleiades: "The Glasswing Butterfly"
Ploughshares: " Reprieve"
Raleigh Review: "The Chokecherry Path" and "The Cloud Path"
Stray Magazine: "The First to Change"
Terrain: "Owl Nest" and "The Mother Tree"
Whitefish Review: "Sleeping with the Eagles"
Willow Springs: "The Week of Moving Glass," "Searching for the Glasses You Dropped in the Creek," "Rereading *Psychic Self-Defense*," "An Ascetic Impulse Surfaces, Tears Leaves from their Stems" and "The Willow Path"

"The Aspen Path" and "Cliff Lake" appeared in the anthology *Poetics for the More-than-Human World*, edited by Mary Newell, Bernard Quetchenbach, and Sarah Nolan.

"An Ascetic Impulse Surfaces, Tears Leaves from their Stems" was featured on *Verse Daily*.

"Sleeping with the Cedars" appeared on *Poetry Daily*, in the series "Eco-poetry Now" (Sally Keith, editor).

Many thanks to the University of Utah's Taft-Nicholson Environmental Humanities Center for my residency in the magnificent Centennial Valley of Montana.

I am endebted to the Academy of American Poets for the Poet Laureate Fellowship, which provided me time to complete many of these poems.

Gratitude and love to my generous preceptors and first readers: Bryher Herak, Robert Baker, Rusty Morrison, Christopher Howell, and Mandy Smoker Broaddus.

May all good things come to you.

MELISSA KWASNY is the author of seven books of poetry, including *Where Outside the Body Is the Soul Today*, *Pictograph*, and *The Nine Senses*, as well as *Earth Recitals: Essays on Image and Vision*. She is also the editor of the anthologies *I Go to the Ruined Place: Contemporary Poets in Defense of Global Human Rights* and *Toward the Open Field: Poets on the Art of Poetry 1800–1950*. Her nonfiction book, *Putting on the Dog: The Animal Origins of What We Wear*, explores the cultural, labor, and environmental histories of clothing materials provided by animals. Kwasny is the recipient of the Poetry Society of America's Cecil Hemley Memorial Award and the Alice Fay Di Castagnola Award. Widely published in anthologies, most recently *Queer Nature*, *Poetics for the More-Than-Human World*, and *The Arcadia Project: North American Postmodern Pastoral*, she is a former Montana Poet Laureate.

milkweed
EDITIONS

Founded as a nonprofit organization in 1980,
Milkweed Editions is an independent publisher. Our mission
is to identify, nurture, and publish transformative literature
and build an engaged community around it.

Milkweed Editions is based in Bdé Óta Othúŋwe (Minneapolis)
within Mní Sota Makhóčhe, the traditional homeland of
the Dakhóta people. Residing here since time immemorial,
Dakhóta people still call Mní Sota Makhóčhe home, with four
federally recognized Dakhóta nations and many more Dakhóta
people residing in what is now the state of Minnesota. Due to
continued legacies of colonization, genocide, and forced removal,
generations of Dakhóta people remain disenfranchised from their
traditional homeland. Presently, Mní Sota Makhóčhe has become
a refuge and home for many Indigenous nations and peoples,
including seven federally recognized Ojibwe nations. We humbly
encourage our readers to reflect upon the historical legacies held
in the lands they occupy.

milkweed.org

Milkweed Editions, an independent nonprofit literary publisher, gratefully acknowledges sustaining support from our board of directors, the McKnight Foundation, the National Endowment for the Arts, and many generous contributions from foundations, corporations, and thousands of individuals—our readers. This activity is made possible by the voters of Minnesota through a Minnesota State Arts Board Operating Support grant, thanks to a legislative appropriation from the arts and cultural heritage fund.

Interior design by Mary Austin Speaker
Typeset in Bembo

Bembo was created in the 1920s under the direction
of printing historian Stanley Morison for the Monotype
Corporation. Bembo is based upon the 1495 design cut by
Francesco Griffo for Aldus Manutius, and named after the first
book to use the typeface, a small book called *De Aetna*, by the
Italian poet and cleric Pietro Bembo.

Printed in the USA
CPSIA information can be obtained
at www.ICGtesting.com
JSHW021655070324
58612JS00001B/1